WITHDRAWN

Noran Bang
The Yellow Room

by
M. J. Kang

Playwrights Canada Press
Toronto Canada

**We acknowledge the support of The Canada Council for the Arts
for our publishing programme
and the Ontario Arts Council**

Cover Photograph by Greg Tjepkema
Cover design by Jodi Armstrong

Canadian Cataloguing in Publication Data

Kang, M.J. (Myung Jin)
  Noran bang the yellow room

A play
ISBN 0-88754-571-8

PS8571.A437N67 1999   C812'.54   C99-931065-8
PR9199.3.K35N67 1999

First edition: June, 1999
Printed and bound by Hignell Printing at Winnipeg, Manitoba, Canada.

dedicated to the memory of

Lance Koyata

M. J. Kang is a playwright and actor based in Toronto. Her plays include *Blessings* (Tarragon Theatre), *Hee Hee: Tales From the White Diamond Mountain* (Blyth Festival Theatre), *Simply Fred* (Toronto Fringe Festival), and *Questioning Condoms* (Rubarb! Buddies in Bad Times Theatre). She has been playwright-in-residence at Nightwood Theatre and Cahoots Theatre Projects, as well as a member of the Tarragon/Chalmers Playwrights Unit, the Theatre Passe Muraille Playwrights Group, and the Banff Playwrights Colony. As an actor, she played Beck Snow on the CBC series *Riverdale*.

Playwright's Notes

Noran Bang: The Yellow Room was written through partial memories and dreams, and what I imagined it might have been like for my family to be in Canada during the early years. Before I started writing *Noran Bang*, I went on long walks, thinking about what to write. After one such walk, I came home with an image of my mother sitting by a kitchen table, crying; my grandmother had just passed away. In many ways, the play wrote itself.

I have chosen to have the same actor play multiple roles because I believe each character the actor plays is an extention of her main character. For example, the actor who plays Umma also plays White Dog. Umma is an explosion waiting to go off. She has a lot of conflicting emotions that are mixed with a great need for justice and righteousness. White Dog, an older character, has seen much in his lifetime and provides a wonderful counter-balance to the Umma character. He doesn't have to prove anything, though he is willing to do anything for love.

Please feel free to cast according to your own vision of the play. The play contains Korean words and phrases, followed by their English translation in square brackets. As a child, I grew up with both Korean and English, and in many ways believed they were one language. Many people may not feel the same way, so do substitute the English translation if necessary.

Noran Bang was developed with the assistance of the Banff Playwright's Colony and the Toronto Arts Council, under the guidance of Kim McCaw; and with the assistance of the Ontario Arts Council during my playwright-in-residency at Cahoots Theatre, under the patient and kind guidance of Marion de Vries.

A great deal of thank yous are extended to Marion de Vries, Woo-Suk Kang, Chun-Ja Kang, Jin-Kyung Kang, Yun-Suk Kang, Tony Rauch-berger, David Rubinoff, Dilara Ally, Lynda Hill, Jane Luk, Jacoba Kaanapa, Stephania Joy, Dave Carley, Jean Yoon, and the Board of Cahoots Theatre Projects.

Production History

Noran Bang: The Yellow Room was first produced in 1993 by Cahoot Theatre Projects, in association with Theatre Passe Muraille, as part of the *3-D Festival: Three Daring New Works by Writers of Diverse Cultures* presented at Theatre Passe Muraille's Backspace, Toronto. The cast and crew of that production were as follows:

MEE-GYUNG KYUNG-MEI HALMONEE	Shelly Hong
HARABOGEE GYUNG-JUNE KYUNG-MA (age 12)	M. J. Kang
KOREAN DRUMMER	Mrs. Kim
APBA (SUNG HEE-GYU) HYUCK-DONG EDWARD MAN	Lance Koyata
UMMA (KYUNG-MA) WHITE DOG KIM JAE KYU PARK CHUNG HEE NORTH KOREAN SOLDIER SOUTH KOREAN SOLDIER	Jean Yoon

Director	Marion de Vries
Set and Lighting Design	An Ge Zhang
Costumes	Jocelyn Hublau
Props	Timothy Hill
Choreography	Xing Bang Fu
Producers	Lynda Hill and Jean Yoon
Production Manager	Andrea Lundy
Production Stage Manager	Cheryl Francis
Stage Manager	Ellen Flowers
Carpenter	Will Sutton

An altered version of *Noran Bang* was produced in 1998 by Cahoots Theatre Projects at the Factory Studio Cafe, Toronto. The cast and crew of that production were as follows:

APBA (SUNG HEE-GYU) HYUCK-DONG EDWARD MAN NORTH KOREAN SOLDIER SOUTH KOREAN SOLDIER	Denis Akiyama
GYUNG-JUNE KYUNG-MA (age 12) HARABOGEE	Marjorie Chan
KOREAN DRUMMER	Charles Hong
MEE-GYUNG KYUNG-MEI HALMONEE	Shelly Hong
UMMA (KYUNG-MA) WHITE DOG	Jean Yoon

Director	David Oiye
Set Design	Kelly Wolf
Lighting Design	Jeff Logue
Costumes	Cecile Belec
Choreography	Jamie Baik
Producer	Maria Costa
Production Manager	David James
Stage Manager	Marla Friedman
Assistant Stage Manager	Alexa Carroll
Painter	Joanne Thompson
Carpenters	Matt Farrell
	Sandra Janzen
	Doug Morum

Noran Bang: The Yellow Room was nominated for a Dora Mavor Moore Award in 1998, for Outstanding New Play in the independent-theatre category.

Exerpts from *Noran Bang* were previously published in *Fireweed* magazine (Spring 1994, no. 43) and the Playwrights Canada Press collections *Beyond the Pale* (1996) and *Taking the Stage* (1994).

The Characters

KYUNG-MA, who is called UMMA ("Mother")

SUNG HEE-GYU, who is called APBA ("Father")

GYUNG-JUNE and MEE-GYUNG, their daughters

HYUCK-DONG, a cousin in Korea

EDWARD, a Canadian boy

WHITE DOG, Gyung-June's dog in Korea

HALMONEE ("Grandmother"), Umma's mother in Korea

HARABOGEE ("Grandfather"), Umma's father in Korea

KYUNG-MA (Umma), as a 12-year-old girl in Korea

KYUNG-MEI, Umma's younger brother in Korea

SOUTH KOREAN SOLDIER

NORTH KOREAN SOLDIER

MAN

The play is set in Toronto in the 1970s and Korea in the past.

Act One

Scene 1

*A slide collage is projected onto the
stage, depicting the family together in
Korea and Canada, as* UMMA *(the
mother),* GYUNG-JUNE, *and* MEE-
GYUNG *(the daughters) perform a
Korean folk dance on stage.* APBA *(the
father) plays the Korean hour-glass
drum, and another drummer plays off
stage. As the dance reaches its climax, a
slide of* HALMONEE *(the grandmother)
appears on stage.*

Scene 2

UMMA is alone on stage, crying.

UMMA   Ahh-u! Ahh-u!

Her daughter, MEE-GYUNG, *enters
hesitantly.*

MEE-GYUNG   Umma? Umma, I'm sorry. Umma?

MEE-GYUNG also starts crying.

UMMA   Halmonee. Halmonee dor-ah-cah-suhut-soh-yoh!
Halmonee dor-ah-cah-suhut-soh-yoh!
[Grandmother has died! Grandmother has died!]

*Her other daughter,·GYUNG-JUNE,
enters as if in a trance.*

GYUNG-JUNE	Umma. I had a dream. Grandmother is dead. We were in a battlefield and she gave me a red flower. Everything else was black and white. She kissed me with a blood flower and told me to be strong. Then she walked along a line—a white line on the ground—to a farm. The farm was on the line. Her hair shed to the ground and her clothes became full of bullets. I couldn't kiss her. I was holding onto her, but I couldn't touch her. She flew me a rose—a white rose—and told me to love this country. She wants to hold me, Umma. She can't die unless I hold her.
UMMA	Moo-seun mal-ee-yah! [What are you saying?]
MEE-GYUNG	Grandmother's dead? Where is she?
GYUNG-JUNE	In Korea.
MEE-GYUNG	Korea?
APBA	*(offstage)* Yo bau. [Darling.]
UMMA	Your father.
GYUNG-JUNE	I want to go back to Korea.

UMMA*'s husband,* APBA, *enters.*

APBA	Yo bau! [Darling!]
GYUNG-JUNE	I need to go back to Korea.
UMMA	*(referring to* APBA*)* He tells me we have no money to see my mother buried. No money to go anywhere.
APBA	Yo bau, come here now!
GYUNG-JUNE	I'm going back on my own!

UMMA *slaps* GYUNG-JUNE.

UMMA	Selfish child!

UMMA *exits.*

MEE-GYUNG	Cah [sister], why'd she hit you?

Pause.

GYUNG-JUNE	Grandmother is dead.

Scene 3

UMMA *and* APBA *in their bedroom.*

APBA	Stop crying. Crying doesn't help. *(passing her a roll of toilet paper)* Here.
UMMA	Am I supposed to shit my tears?
APBA	Come back to bed.
UMMA	Why won't you let me go?
APBA	It's late. Time to sleep.
UMMA	You made me come here. You made me pack my bags and travel to this—this place!
APBA	Shee-guh-ruh-wuhoo! [Better be quiet!]

UMMA *lies down beside him, with her back to him.*

Sleep well.

Scene 4

> MEE-GYUNG *and* GYUNG-JUNE*'s bedroom.* GYUNG-JUNE *is crying and* MEE-GYUNG *is staring at the ceiling.*

MEE-GYUNG   Cah, what happened tonight?

GYUNG-JUNE   Halmonee promised to be with me. Always.

MEE-GYUNG   Oh.

GYUNG-JUNE   Why were you crying?

MEE-GYUNG   Umma was crying.

GYUNG-JUNE   Do you even remember Halmonee?

MEE-GYUNG   No. Am I bad for not remembering?

GYUNG-JUNE   No. You were young when we left. Only four years old. Everyone loved you because you were so quiet. Not as loud as our cousin. Do you remember Hyuck-Dong?

> *Flashback to Korea: Their cousin,* HYUCK-DONG, *is in the yard of a small house, giving commands to* WHITE DOG.

HYUCK-DONG   Sit down. I said "Sit!" Listen to me!

GYUNG-JUNE   He annoyed everyone and kept on trying to hurt my dog.

> HYUCK-DONG *prods* WHITE DOG *with a stick.*

HYUCK-DONG   I'll poke you until you sit. Do you like being poked?

WHITE DOG   I hate you, jerk!

GYUNG-JUNE	Remember the dog I had?
MEE-GYUNG	The big white one?
GYUNG-JUNE	Yes. White Dog.

> HYUCK-DONG *whacks the ground with the stick.*

HYUCK-DONG	I'm not scared by you!
WHITE DOG	I haven't shown you my teeth yet!

> *He shows* HYUCK-DONG *his teeth.* GYUNG-JUNE *exits from the house.*

GYUNG-JUNE	Hyuck-Dong! Leave my dog alone!
WHITE DOG	(*to* GYUNG-JUNE) Let me bite him. Right on his bum.
HYUCK-DONG	Hey, what's he saying?
WHITE DOG	One little bite. Right there. Left cheek. Bull's eye!
GYUNG-JUNE	(*to* WHITE DOG) No. I'll get in trouble.
HYUCK-DONG	(*to* GYUNG-JUNE) Your dog is stupid!
GYUNG-JUNE	(*to* HYUCK-DONG) You're stupid!
HYUCK-DONG	You're stupid! And that dog is stu-pi-dest! He can't respect that I am the smar-test!

> HALMONEE *enters the stage without being noticed.*

GYUNG-JUNE	My dog is smarter than you. My dog is smarter because he knows you are a bad person, a bad person he won't play with—he's not *allowed* to play with!

HYUCK-DONG　What do you mean—"Not allowed to play with?"

GYUNG-JUNE　'Cause I said so.

WHITE DOG　Uh oh.

HYUCK-DONG　Your mother said I can play with him whenever I want. Your mother said he's my dog too! You mother said I get everything of yours because we're cousins!

GYUNG-JUNE　He's my dog!

HALMONEE　Shee-guh-ruh! [Too noisy!]

GYUNG-JUNE　Halmonee, Hyuck-Dong tried to kill my dog!

HALMONEE　Gyung-June-na, everything is okay. Come inside and have yummy ducc gouk [rice cake soup].

GYUNG-JUNE　You put some mandu [pork dumplings] too?

HALMONEE　Yes, my special dumplings for my only Gyung-June. Hyuck-Dong, you may join us after you finish tying up the dog and take a bath. Nem-say-nah! [You smell bad.]

WHITE DOG　Hey! Steal some mandu for me too—okay, Gyung-June?

　　　　　HYUCK-DONG *drags poor* WHITE DOG *to be tied up.*

GYUNG-JUNE　*(to* MEE-GYUNG*)* That's how Grandmother was. Even when I wasn't the saint, she took my side.

MEE-GYUNG　Halmonee liked me too, right?

GYUNG-JUNE　Yes, but I was her favourite.

MEE-GYUNG　White Dog liked me best though.

GYUNG-JUNE	He was my dog!
MEE-GYUNG	I liked him. He was my friend too. Cah, how come they're in Korea and we're in Canada?
GYUNG-JUNE	Because of you. You screwed everything up.
MEE-GYUNG	Really?
GYUNG-JUNE	We just came here and they stayed there.
MEE-GYUNG	I miss White Dog.

They both fall asleep.

Scene 5

Flashback to Korea: UMMA *and* APBA *perform a courtship dance.* APBA *exits and* UMMA *is left sitting alone, drinking coffee in a cafe, waiting.* APBA *rushes in.*

APBA	Kyung-Ma?
UMMA	Sung Hee-Gyu?
APBA	Yes. Your picture—it doesn't do you justice. You are much prettier in person.
UMMA	Thanks. You're late.
APBA	Sorry. Would you like anything?
UMMA	Look, I only came here because my mother and my oldest sister told me I should.
APBA	*(sitting down)* Well... why don't you tell me something about yourself?

UMMA I work as an assistant calculus professor. It's part of my doctorate. I plan to finish my Ph.D. in the next couple of years and start working full-time. I am the youngest of six children—three boys and three girls. My oldest sister and my mother think you would be a good match for me, but I am not planning to date until I finish my Ph.D. Your turn.

APBA I studied theology in university, but because of my parents' financial situation, I switched my major to business. I work at the Bank of Korea, as a manager. I recently got promoted. I am the youngest as well. Of five. One girl and four boys. All live in Seoul, except my oldest brother who lives in Canada and my second oldest brother who lives in North Korea. They both chose to live in the different countries after the war. *(beat)* Do you have a problem with my brother living in North Korea?

UMMA It was his choice. Why would it bother me?

APBA Do you see it as being shameful? Do you pity me?

UMMA No. I am ashamed of what happened during and after the war. What was the point of the Korean War? Death? Further separation? Devastation everywhere? Who won the war? Russia and the United States. Who lost the war? Koreans. Who do I pity? Anyone who believes one regime is better than the other. North Korea has Kim Il Song. South Korea has Park Chung Hee. We both have dictators as our government head. How can anyone say one is better?

APBA Boy, you're really passionate about politics.

UMMA People have to take responsibility for their government, for who they elect or who leads them. No one is powerless. *(checks her watch)* Sorry, I have to go.

She gets up to leave.

APBA We sat and talked. We know a little bit about each other. Now we can leave. It was nice meeting you. *(also gets up to leave, then stops)* Look, I find you attractive, interesting, and you're obviously intelligent... so...?

UMMA So...?

APBA So why don't you give me a chance?

Pause.

UMMA What took you so long?

APBA Why was I late today?

UMMA The picture. My sister gave your sister-in-law the picture of me to give to you a month ago. It took you a month to decide if I was worth dating?

APBA When I was first given your picture, I wanted to call you right away, but then I thought I should wait until I got my promotion. So I could impress you. I guess I don't impress you.

UMMA It would have been good if you were on time. Today.

APBA I was figuring out what to wear. Do I look good?

Pause.

UMMA Do you like movies?

APBA Yes.

UMMA Well?

APBA Well what?

UMMA	Ask me to go to a movie.
APBA	Would you like to go to a movie?
UMMA	Next week? Saturday? Evening show? You'll pick me up at my place at six so we can walk to the theatre. And talk some more?
APBA	How would you like to go to a movie... next week Saturday? And I could even pick you up at your place around... six... if that's all right with you.
UMMA	It was nice meeting you. I'm sorry, but I do have to rush off. I made an appointment to tutor someone. I didn't think we would be long.
APBA	Your appointment—is it far from here?
UMMA	A few blocks.
APBA	Would you mind if I walked you?
UMMA	No, not at all.

They start to walk off stage.

APBA	Just a question—how many children would you like to have... one day... with whomever you marry?
UMMA	Two. One boy and one girl. How many would you like?
APBA	Two is a nice number.

Scene 6

Flashback to Korea: The home of
HALMONEE *and* HARABOGEE,
UMMA's *parents.*

HARABOGEE   I understand you want to ask me something.

APBA   Yes.

HARABOGEE   Go on then.

APBA   I would like— I would like—

HALMONEE   This is so wonderful.

APBA   I would like your daughter's hand in marriage...
if you please.

HARABOGEE   My daughter is stubborn.

UMMA   *(to her father)* Apba.

HARABOGEE   And pig-headed.

UMMA   Apba.

HARABOGEE   She does what she wishes. She took after her
mother.

HALMONEE   Yo bau! [Darling!]

HARABOGEE   Do you think you can handle a lifetime of this?

APBA   I would love to.

HARABOGEE   Well then... congratulations on your
engagement. It would be best to wait before you
have children.

Scene 7

> *In a schoolyard, during lunch time.*
> GYUNG-JUNE *is sitting by herself,*
> *quietly singing "Ah Ree Rang."*
> HALMONEE *is standing above her,*
> *humming along, and* GYUNG-JUNE*'s*
> *singing underscores* HALMONEE*'s*
> *words. ["Ah-Ree-Rang" loosely*
> *translates as: "I'll always be with you*
> *no matter how far the walk, or even if*
> *my feet hurt."]*

HALMONEE When you sing these words, remember the times we've shared in Korea. Don't forget where you're from. Don't forget me, Gyung-June-na.

> HALMONEE *exits as* GYUNG-JUNE
> *finishes the song.* EDWARD *enters*
> *with his lunch.*

EDWARD Gi-ung... June? Am I saying it right?

GYUNG-JUNE Edward, everyone calls me June. Okay!

EDWARD Sorry. So, June, what do you have for lunch?

GYUNG-JUNE What do you have for your lunch?

EDWARD Tuna fish. Every day—tuna fish. My mom thinks I love tuna fish. I can't stand tuna fish.

GYUNG-JUNE What do you do with it?

EDWARD The tuna fish? Eat it. I get hungry. C'mon, tell me what you have for lunch.

GYUNG-JUNE You really want to know?

EDWARD I'm curious about you.

GYUNG-JUNE My mom packs me bap [rice] and kimchi [pickled cabbage] with other pan-chan [side dishes].

EDWARD	Huh?
GYUNG-JUNE	In English, they call it rice. "Bap" is rice. "Kimchi" is—it's smelly food, so I don't like eating it around other people.
EDWARD	Is that why you sit alone at lunch?
GYUNG-JUNE	So?
EDWARD	It's just that I want to sit with you.
GYUNG-JUNE	Really?
EDWARD	Gi-ung-June—June— I like your real name.
GYUNG-JUNE	You do? How come?
EDWARD	It's beautiful. Like you.
GYUNG-JUNE	I'm beautiful?
EDWARD	Sure, why not?
GYUNG-JUNE	I like you, Edward.
EDWARD	Gi-ung-June, can I call you Gi-ung-June?
GYUNG-JUNE	Sure.
EDWARD	Gi-ung-June, I came to ask you a favour. I... um... well, my friend likes this person, but he doesn't know if she likes him. What do I do? I mean, how does my friend find out if she likes him.
GYUNG-JUNE	Well, first you must tell me who your friend likes.
EDWARD	Patty.
GYUNG-JUNE	Patty?

EDWARD	She's cute.
GYUNG-JUNE	Patty and I are friends.
EDWARD	She's really cute.
GYUNG-JUNE	Edward, did you really mean it when you said I'm beautiful?
EDWARD	Sure. Do you know if she likes me?
GYUNG-JUNE	Many people like you, Edward.
EDWARD	Thanks. You're great, Gi-ung-June.

MEE-GYUNG *enters.*

MEE-GYUNG	Cah, can I eat lunch with you? I'm mad at Michelle.
GYUNG-JUNE	No!
MEE-GYUNG	She told me I can't be her friend.
GYUNG-JUNE	Leave me alone!
EDWARD	Is this your little sister?
GYUNG-JUNE	No. Yeah. My bratty sister.

EDWARD *stands up to greet* MEE-GYUNG.

EDWARD	Nice to meet you, little sister of Gi-ung-June.

MEE-GYUNG *starts laughing, pointing at* EDWARD*'s crotch. His zipper is open.*

GYUNG-JUNE	Mee-Gyung!
EDWARD	Excuse me. *(turns around and fixes his zipper)* Your sister looks at interesting body parts.

GYUNG-JUNE	She can't help it. It's where her eye level is.
EDWARD	*(to* MEE-GYUNG*)* You think that's funny, huh? You think that's funny?
MEE-GYUNG	Yeah! Very funny!
EDWARD	Let's see if you think this is funny! *(he starts tickling* MEE-GYUNG*)* Hey, want a piggy back ride?
MEE-GYUNG	Sure!
EDWARD	C'mon, hop on! It'll be my way to thank you for telling me I was flying low.
	MEE-GYUNG *hops on his back, and they exit as if he is an airplane and she is his passenger.*
MEE-GYUNG	Vroom, vroom. Zoooommmmm!
GYUNG-JUNE	*(with adolescent sexual angst)* I noticed his fly was open too.

Scene 8

	MEE-GYUNG *is sitting in her room, playing with her truck, halfheartedly.* APBA *enters.*
APBA	There you are. Usually when I come home for dinner, you're running to my side, ready to lie down on my stomach. Aren't you going to ask if I have any cho-co-late?
MEE-GYUNG	Apba, I'm not going back to school. Ever.
APBA	You know education is very important. Now, guess what's in this bag.

MEE-GYUNG	Apba, I can't go to school anymore.
APBA	What is happening in Mee-Gyung's life?
MEE-GYUNG	I'm in trouble. You can't tell Umma, okay? I hit someone at school today. *(APBA laughs)* Why are you laughing?
APBA	You are always hitting someone.
MEE-GYUNG	Stop laughing! Listen, okay. I'm telling you a secret.

> APBA *puts his finger to his mouth as a promise of silence.*

Michelle told me I had a rip in my pants, right where my gung-deong-ee is. *(gestures to her bum)* Not only that, but she told everyone in class. And they asked to see my hole. Then, when the teacher asked what was going on, I farted. Michelle said coloured gas came out of my bum. The teacher yelled at me to go to the office. Only me. So I hit Michelle.

> MEE-GYUNG *takes an envelope from her pocket.*

Now I have to get this signed, and there's a meeting with the principal you have to go to.

APBA	*(laughing)* You are the son I never had.
MEE-GYUNG	You're weird.

Scene 9

UMMA *is alone on stage, sleeping, and has a dream:*

GYUNG-JUNE   *(offstage)* Kyung-Ma, tell me a story.

GYUNG-JUNE *enters.*

UMMA   Gyung-June-na, let me tell you a story.

GYUNG-JUNE   About Halmonee?

UMMA   No. Once upon a time, there was a younger brother—Kyung-Mei. *(MEE-GYUNG comes on stage as KYUNG-MEI)* And an older sister by three years—Kyung-Ma.

KYUNG-MEI *gives* GYUNG-JUNE *a shirt, and* GYUNG-JUNE *becomes* KYUNG-MA.

UMMA   This was Kyung-Mei's favourite story.

KYUNG-MA   Once upon a time, the family owned an enchanted farm. The farm was enchanted because it was built on land given to one of our ancestors by the king of Korea, back when Korea was governed by monarchy. This ancestor of ours built this farm so future generations of his family could grow and prosper. Do you know why the king gave land to our ancestors?

KYUNG-MEI   Because this ancestor was the king's court jester, who in reality was the best trained assassin in Korea. Kyung-Ma, tell me how the court jester killed the king's enemies. Tell me about the man who ate all the kimchi.

KYUNG-MA   Kyung-Mei, are you sure you want to hear that story again?

KYUNG-MEI   Yes. Massive quantities of kimchi....

KYUNG-MA	Massive quantities of kimchi were disappearing from all round the country. Everyone became worried. With no kimchi, who could eat their rice? One month of investigations went by. And still no one found the kimchi. Two months of investigations went by, and it still remained a mystery. All around the country, people were fainting because there was no kimchi! Finally, the king asked his dear court jester—our ancestor—to please use his smarts to find the kimchi. During investigations, our ancestor found out who the abductor was. Normally a person of such menace would be hanged, but the court jester asked the king to invite this low life for some entertainment. At first the king refused.
KYUNG-MEI	Such a man would taint the great tradition of torture.
KYUNG-MA	But the court jester ensured the king that this was the only way to get the kimchi back. So, as the low life sat laughing at the entertainment provided by the court jester, he noticed his stomach growing—
KYUNG-MEI	Until it exploded, popping his belly and exposing all the kimchi he had eaten!
KYUNG-MA	And everybody lived happily ever after because they had kimchi to go with their rice.
KYUNG-MEI	And to reward the court jester, the king gave him land.
KYUNG-MA	With that land, the court jester built a farm and lived happily ever after.
KYUNG-MEI	What happened to the farm? You've never told me that part.
KYUNG-MA	What is there to tell? When you were inside Umma's belly, the family was forced to leave the farm.

KYUNG-MEI	Why?
KYUNG-MA	Some people don't believe in having homes, so they take them away from others out of jealousy. That's why soldiers wear green.
KYUNG-MEI	Huh?
KYUNG-MA	Our home was on a line. A stupid parallel where no man can live. The D.M.Z. It doesn't make sense to me either.
KYUNG-MEI	We have to get the farm back.
KYUNG-MA	It is the most beautiful farm. Ever. When we get to it, you have to close your eyes. I want it to be a surprise.
	They close their eyes. A SOUTH KOREAN SOLDIER *enters.*
SOLDIER	*(grabbing* KYUNG-MA*'s arm)* Hey, what are you doing here? This is no place for children. Go home.
KYUNG-MA	We're going home.
SOLDIER	Here? What home?
	KYUNG-MA *slowly becomes* GYUNG-JUNE *again.*
KYUNG-MEI	Our home. The king gave the land to the court jester.
SOLDIER	This is the D.M.Z. The demilitarized zone. No Man's Land.
KYUNG-MEI	But the war is over.
SOLDIER	It will never be over. Go home, your parents will worry.

UMMA
And so, Gyung-June-na—Kyung-Ma, and Kyung-Mei went home to their parents, but promised to return to their real home. One day.

GYUNG-JUNE
Umma, I don't want to hear your stories.

>GYUNG-JUNE *exits.* KYUNG-MEI *sees a stick, picks it up, and pretends it is a gun.* UMMA *sees this and slowly walks away.*

Scene 10

>*Early morning in* APBA *and* UMMA's *bedroom.* APBA *is about to leave for work. He sits on the bed, stroking* UMMA's *hair as she sleeps.*

APBA
Sleep. What are you dreaming about? Dreaming of a time when everything went well? We have two beautiful children. We don't live in shambles. It's only been five years. Time is all we need. Remember when you passed your English course and you said to me, "I am a true Canadian. I can read and write the word 'maple leaf'." I remember your smile, your laughter, your willingness to begin anew. Where did it go? Where is the lady who enchanted me by her determination? I miss her. She has become empty. You gave up. Left me to hold the family. I'm trying. But it's hard when you have no support. Bank manager turns waiter, as he crosses the ocean into the new world. *(snaps his fingers, imitating a restaurant customer)* "Mr. Chinaman! Mr. Chinaman!" That is what they call me at work: "Mr. Chinaman." And I nod and smile, pretending I do not hear. It is better that way. Is that what you do when I talk to you? Because you never seem to listen.

Scene 11

> *Flashback to Korea:* APBA *and* UMMA's *home.* UMMA *is alone as* APBA *enters.*

APBA   I am home!

UMMA   Shhhh. Mee-Gyung is finally asleep. She was crying a lot today. I think she's teething. How was your day?

APBA   Good. I stopped by somewhere on my way home. Would you like to know where I stopped by?

UMMA   You stopped by the grocery store and picked up what I asked you to pick up. For dinner?

APBA   I forgot.

UMMA   Hope you don't mind ramen then.

APBA   Stop. Relax. Close your eyes. Stick out your hand.

> *As* UMMA *does so,* APBA *takes a jewellery box from his pocket. As he opens the box, she opens her eyes and sees a pearl necklace.*

UMMA   It's very beautiful.

APBA   Put it on.

UMMA   Why?

APBA   Because I bought it for you to put it on!

UMMA   Why the gift?

APBA   Can't I give my wife presents? Here. Let me put it on for you.

He takes the necklace from the box and puts it on her.

Turn around. You are so beautiful. Look in the mirror. How was your day today?

UMMA   Busy.

APBA   How was your meeting?

UMMA   Like any other meeting.

APBA   What did you talk about at the meeting?

UMMA   The new budget—where we are going to allot the funds. Fairly boring discussion.

APBA   Tell me, why is it that every time you have "a meeting with the faculty," I hear from other people that you were at a protest. At all the protests against the government? How long has this been going on?

UMMA   Why don't you tell me?

APBA   Yo bau, I don't want to fight. Why don't you tell me these things?

UMMA   You know what the government is doing to the Korean people—all under the guise of democracy. And you don't care.

APBA   I care about my family. About my wife. I care about— Yo bau, I've been thinking. Korea isn't safe for us anymore. And demonstrating against the government doesn't help that much either, does it?

UMMA   It helps more than doing nothing.

APBA   Do you really believe that?

UMMA   Isn't it our duty as Koreans to fight for what we believe? Park Chung Hee is a totalitarian. How can we tolerate such a leader?

APBA   My duty is for the safety and prosperity of my family. I don't know if it's possible to grow here. There are too many political rules and regulations. And it won't change. Not for a long time. They want to promote me. The bank wants to promote me to vice president of international operations.

UMMA   That's wonderful.

APBA   There is a condition. Not a condition—a normal procedural practice. To go through my family lineage to make sure I am of good blood. They will find out about my brother. My brother in North Korea. When they find out, I will be fired.

UMMA   But it's not your fault...

Pause.

What are you going to do?

APBA   I've been talking to my father, and he thinks the best thing for us to do is to move away, move away to another country. My eldest brother in Toronto is willing to sponsor us. We can start over. Canada is a country full of opportunities.

What is going to happen when either Gyung-June or Mee-Gyung are up for promotion, and they will be fired because their uncle lives in North Korea? Can you live with the knowledge that we limited their lives? And what about your involvement with the Student Committee? Don't you realize you are only putting your family in jeopardy?

UMMA   Things are going to change.

APBA	They haven't changed for over twenty-five years.
UMMA	I don't want to leave here.
APBA	And once we're there, we can sponsor some of our relatives. They can start their lives over too. A whole new world of possibilities. Your mother and father can come live with us. In our new home. We can have our own Korea in Canada. It will be best for us. Always do what's best for you.
UMMA	Thank you for the necklace. I don't want to leave.

Scene 12

> *The family kitchen.* MEE-GYUNG *and* GYUNG-JUNE *are playing "Scissors Paper Stone."* UMMA *is cooking.*

GIRLS	Ga-ooee ba-ooee bo! [Scissors, paper, stone!]
MEE-GYUNG	Paper covers stone. I win.
GYUNG-JUNE	No! No! It's best four out of five. You've only won three, you still have to win one more.
GIRLS	Ga-ooee ba-ooee bo!
MEE-GYUNG	Stone crushes scissor. My fourth win.
GYUNG-JUNE	That one doesn't count. I wasn't ready.
MEE-GYUNG	I won. You lost. I get to lie on Apba's stomach when he gets home.
GYUNG-JUNE	No. You cheated.
MEE-GYUNG	I did not.

GYUNG-JUNE   Chinks always cheat.

MEE-GYUNG   Umma, Cah called me a Chink.

UMMA   *(not knowing what "Chink" means)* Don't call her a Chink, Gyung-June.

MEE-GYUNG   *(in a whisper)* What's a Chink?

GYUNG-JUNE   You are. We are. Funny looking people are.

MEE-GYUNG   Why are we funny looking?

GYUNG-JUNE   We're ugly.

MEE-GYUNG   I'm not ugly. I'm going to be... I'm going to be pret-ty.

GYUNG-JUNE   No Chinks are pretty!

MEE-GYUNG   I'll be the first.

GYUNG-JUNE   Not only are you a Chink, but a Chink from a black witch's family. Umma and Apba saw you being thrown out of a gypsy's van, so they took you home because they felt sorry for you. You were so ugly, you were giving the gypsies warts!

MEE-GYUNG   That's not true. Then how come I don't give Mommy and Daddy warts?

GYUNG-JUNE   They took some of my beauty and gave it to you. That's why I'm a Chink too.

MEE-GYUNG   You must have been pret-ty.

GYUNG-JUNE   I was very pret-ty.

MEE-GYUNG   'Cause I'm more pret-tier than you. They gave me too much! Right, Umma?

UMMA   You both are my darlings. Now, no more fighting before dinner.

MEE-GYUNG	Mommy loves me more. 'Cause I'm pret-tier.
GYUNG-JUNE	'Cause you give her the most pain.
MEE-GYUNG	I don't get it.
GYUNG-JUNE	She pretends she loves you more so you'll stop bugging her. Bugger! *(she laughs at MEE-GYUNG and points at her eyes)* You have bug eyes! With no eyelids. Bug eyes! Bug eyes!
MEE-GYUNG	So do you!
GYUNG-JUNE	And you have a flat nose. A flat nose like you bang yourself into walls as a daily sport. And you have thick, coarse, bone-straight hair. Black as the black witches you're from!
MEE-GYUNG	Umma, Cah's scaring me!
GYUNG-JUNE	Stop calling me "Cah"! That's not my name.
MEE-GYUNG	But I have to. It's respect.
GYUNG-JUNE	It's "Kun-uhn-nee"—"Big Sister," not "Cah", like "ca-ca".
MEE-GYUNG	But I always call you "Cah."
GYUNG-JUNE	You're not a baby anymore. You can say "Kun-uhn-nee." Before it was fine, before you were cute, but now you're a Chink. A Chink from black witches!
MEE-GYUNG	I don't like how you talk. You're from black witches too. You! And your lies!
GYUNG-JUNE	Go back to where you belong!
	Pause.
MEE-GYUNG	Do you want to play another game?

GYUNG-JUNE   No. I have homework.

MEE-GYUNG   Cah, how come people are so mean? I was
                  walking from the store today, not doing
                  anything—I promise. But a man came up to me
                  and—

                        Flashback: A MAN *enters.*

MAN   Hey, do you live here?

MEE-GYUNG   Uhhh.... *(shaking her head)* Uh uh.

MAN   What are you doing here?

MEE-GYUNG   Walking to the store.

MAN   How come your feet ain't bound?

MEE-GYUNG   Huh?

MAN   Don't all Chinese girls have their feet bound?

MEE-GYUNG   I'm not Chinese.

MAN   Then what are you?

MEE-GYUNG   None of your business!

MAN   Go back to where you came from!

                        As the MAN *starts to walk away,* MEE-
                        GYUNG *punches him on the back.*

MEE-GYUNG   This is my home!

                        The Man grabs her, but MEE-GYUNG
                        kicks him and runs back to GYUNG-
                        JUNE.

GYUNG-JUNE   Were you with anyone?

MEE-GYUNG   My friend Michelle. No, I was by myself.

GYUNG-JUNE	What were you doing by yourself?
MEE-GYUNG	I found a quarter and wanted candy.
GYUNG-JUNE	You don't talk to strangers. Okay!
MEE-GYUNG	Yes.
GYUNG-JUNE	And you don't hit strangers. Okay!
MEE-GYUNG	I got angry. How come I hit him? I didn't mean to. It was just... what do you call it?
GYUNG-JUNE	Reflexes?
MEE-GYUNG	Yes. Re-flec-sives-sives. My arm. It has re-flec-sives-sives.
GYUNG-JUNE	The man was stupid. Next time, ask me to go to the store. Okay? *(MEE-GYUNG nods her head)* Little sister, let's play "Thumb War."
MEE-GYUNG	I hit him hard.
GYUNG-JUNE	Good.
	APBA enters, as MEE-GYUNG *and* GYUNG-JUNE *start to play.*
MEE-GYUNG	One, two, three, four, I declare a thumb war. Bow and kiss. You have to bow and kiss! Bow and kiss.
UMMA	*(to* APBA*)* Park Chung Hee was on the Korean radio again. Spewing about the good he has done for "Democratic Korea," the good he has done for the people of his nation. When is that man ever going to shut up and die? *(APBA laughs)* Why are you laughing?
APBA	It's good to see that passion. Hello.
UMMA	Hello to you too.

They sit together.

APBA   I made some very good tips today. To put into our savings. One day, we will have everything we've ever dreamt about.

UMMA   One day. In this country.

APBA   In our country. One day, when we are rich. *(pause)* How was your day?

UMMA   Good.

APBA   How are you feeling?

UMMA   Better.

APBA   What did you do today to make yourself feel better?

UMMA   I had a nice talk with my sister.

APBA   Your sister?

UMMA   Yes, I called her.

APBA   You called her? You called her long distance?

UMMA   It was short.

APBA   When?

UMMA   What?

APBA   When did you call her?

UMMA   Today. Sometime during the day.

APBA   What time?

UMMA   I don't know. Around three. Maybe three—three o'clock.

APBA	No discount! No discount!
UMMA	She said the family will pay half if I want to visit my mother's grave.
APBA	With what money? They paid for the funeral and the burial costs. Now you want to take money from them so you can visit a block of cement? No more long distance.
UMMA	The kids are waiting for you.
APBA	No more long distance.
UMMA	I heard!

APBA *enters the living room area.*

APBA	Mee-Gyung-a, Gyung-June-na?
MEE-GYUNG	Apba, I found a quarter today.
GYUNG-JUNE	And she hit a man on her way to the store.
MEE-GYUNG	Cahh.
GYUNG-JUNE	He was calling her names, and told her she didn't belong here—so she hit him.
APBA	Is that true?
MEE-GYUNG	Is that good or bad, Apba?
APBA	You don't hit people. It is not good to hit.
MEE-GYUNG	But Umma hit Cah.
GYUNG-JUNE	Don't tell him that. I deserved it.
APBA	*(to* UMMA*)* Is this true, yo bau? True that you hit our eldest?

UMMA	It was after our fight. I was upset, Gyung-June was being disrespectful.
APBA	*(to* GYUNG-JUNE*)* Don't give your mother trouble. *(pause)* I learned a Canadian song. Want to hear it?
MEE-GYUNG	Yes. Please. But Apba, do you have anything for us? Cho-co-late? Cho-co-lates?
APBA	Let me look at your teeth. *(with a look of displeasure)* Eshh! Smelly! Have you been brushing them after treats?
MEE-GYUNG	Sometimes. No.
APBA	Why not?
MEE-GYUNG	Cahhh.
GYUNG-JUNE	Because she's too busy playing with her truck... or doing homework.
APBA	Playing with your truck. Hmmm. Wouldn't you rather play with a doll?
MEE-GYUNG	Why? They're ugly. I like trucks.
APBA	Close your eyes. *(he takes out a doll)* Open them.
MEE-GYUNG	It's a doll.
APBA	Do you like it?
MEE-GYUNG	A doll with blond hair and blue eyes. Apba, I can't have it. It can't be part of our family.
APBA	What do you mean?
MEE-GYUNG	It doesn't look like us.
APBA	Who said that?

MEE-GYUNG	Michelle.
APBA	Don't tell her. Leave it at home. Your own secret toy.
MEE-GYUNG	Thank you. Go-mahb-seun-nee-da. [Thank you very much.]

> MEE-GYUNG *bows and holds the doll limply.*

GYUNG-JUNE	Do you have something for me?
APBA	For you, a book. A book about Canada: *Anne of Green Gables.*
GYUNG-JUNE	Go-mahb-seun-nee-da, abogee. [Thank you very much, Father.]

> GYUNG-JUNE *flips through the book.*

APBA	What? You don't like it?
GYUNG-JUNE	Abpa, it's just—next time, can I get a book about Korea?
APBA	I thought you would like *Anne of Green Gables.* The sales lady said all the Canadian school kids read that book.
GYUNG-JUNE	But I'm not Canadian.
APBA	You are now. You will enjoy being Canadian. Now the song. A man I work with sang it today. I said to him, "What a nice song." So he taught me. It has a catchy tune. The man said him and his family sing this song all the time. Okay, listen carefully. *(begins to sing slowly)* "Row, row, row your boat—"
MEE-GYUNG	"—gently down the stream. Merrily, merrily, merrily—"

APBA   Oh, you know it.

MEE-GYUNG   My teacher taught us that one a long time ago.

GYUNG-JUNE   Sing it for us. Please, Apba.

MEE-GYUNG   But you have to lie down on your back first. I
                  won. I get to lie on your stomach.

GYUNG-JUNE   She cheated.

APBA   Cheated—is that true?

GYUNG-JUNE   No. I lost, so I lie on your leg.

                  APBA *lies down on his back.* MEE-
                  GYUNG *lies down and puts her head on
                  his stomach.* GYUNG-JUNE *lies down
                  and puts her head on his right leg. They
                  all sing "Row, Row, Row Your Boat."*

GYUNG-JUNE   That's my favourite song.

MEE-GYUNG   Me too.

                  Lights go down, except on UMMA,
                  *who stands alone, looking pensive.
                  "Ah-Ree-Rang" is drummed lightly
                  offstage, as lights go to black.*

                  End of Act One.

Act Two

Scene 13

> *Early in the morning in* UMMA *and*
> APBA*'s bedroom.* APBA *is getting*
> *ready to go to work.* UMMA *comes*
> *into the bedroom with breakfast.*

UMMA   Man-nee jab-soo-sae-yo. [Please eat a lot.]

APBA   They feed me at work.

UMMA   Junk food.

APBA   Good food. People pay good money for—

UMMA   Junk. They feed you junk. You work so hard, you should eat a proper meal before you go.

APBA   You want something from me.

> UMMA *pauses, as she lays out food.*

UMMA   I've been thinking.... Why are you never home?

APBA   I work. You know how hard I work. I have to pay the bills.

UMMA   We never spend time together. You spend one hour with the children. And children grow up so fast. They miss you.

APBA   We need the money.

UMMA   What if I start to work?

APBA   Who is going to hire you? What kind of job will you get? Your diploma is useless. You can hardly speak the language.

UMMA	I saw a job posting. It's a job at a school—janitorial engineer. Speaking English is not necessary, and they don't care about your education.
APBA	You think you can just apply and they'll hire you? It's not so easy.
UMMA	I want to help. I don't want to stay home all the time. The kids have school during the day. Yo bau, I am so lonely. Please.
APBA	Do what you want to do. Do what's best for yourself.
UMMA	Com-oh-way-oh. [Thanks.]

She bows and exits.

APBA	But know that children need a mother more than they need a father. Especially two girls.

Scene 14

MEE-GYUNG and GYUNG-JUNE in their bedroom.

MEE-GYUNG	Cah? Cah, can I talk with you?
GYUNG-JUNE	I'm busy. I'm reading *Anne of Green Gables*. What do you want?
MEE-GYUNG	I don't know. Just to talk.
GYUNG-JUNE	What do you want to talk about?
MEE-GYUNG	I don't know. What do you want to talk about?
GYUNG-JUNE	Do you miss anything about Korea?
MEE-GYUNG	Should I?

GYUNG-JUNE   You don't care about anyone but yourself. You don't realize how I had to give up everything because of you. If it weren't for you, I would have been able to stay in Korea with Halmonee. You're a brat, and I have to take care of you. Because of you, Halmonee died.

> GYUNG-JUNE *exits.*

Scene 15

> WHITE DOG *enters the children's bedroom.*

WHITE DOG   Meeeeeee-Gyung.

MEE-GYUNG   White Dog? What are you doing in Canada?

WHITE DOG   It got lonely in Korea. It got boring biting Hyuck-Dong, day in and day out.

MEE-GYUNG   Everyone is acting strange. Halmonee died and everyone is sad about it. But I'm not. Should I be?

WHITE DOG   Death is a funny thing. Do you want to be sad?

MEE-GYUNG   Nope.

WHITE DOG   Then don't be.

MEE-GYUNG   I got a new truck. I took it from school. And Apba gave me an ugly doll. Want to see them?

WHITE DOG   Yeah!

> MEE-GYUNG *rushes off stage, then rushes back on with the doll and a big red truck.*

MEE-GYUNG   Vroom, vroom, vroom.

MEE-GYUNG *moves the truck forward, throws the doll in front of the truck, then runs it over.* MEE-GYUNG *looks to* WHITE DOG *to see if what she did was okay.*

WHITE DOG   Do it again!

She backs the truck up and runs the doll over again and again. Then she picks the doll up again.

MEE-GYUNG   *(as the doll)* Help me! Help me! *(backs the truck up and runs the doll over several more times)* Help me! Help me!

MEE-GYUNG *finally kicks the doll offstage.*

WHITE DOG   Good work!

MEE-GYUNG *pushes the truck, and follows it off stage with the doll.*

Scene 16

GYUNG-JUNE *has a nightmare/fantasy:*

HALMONEE   See the colour. What is it? The colour of your face.

EDWARD   Is it light or dark?

GYUNG-JUNE   Light.

HALMONEE   And your eyes.

GYUNG-JUNE   Dark.

HALMONEE   Black. Black almond eyes.

EDWARD	No eyelids. Like a slimy snake's.
HALMONEE	Smooth eyelids to blink back wetness. Salty wetness. I miss you too.
EDWARD	Your eyebrows are in the middle of your forehead.
HALMONEE	They hover over your lashes.
EDWARD	Almost to your hairline.
HALMONEE	Your hair. Black. Straight. Thick.
EDWARD	Coarse.
GYUNG-JUNE	I can't help how I look!
EDWARD	Change your looks to what you want to be.
HALMONEE q	Darling child, you can be anything you want to be.
GYUNG-JUNE	Change so Edward will like me?
HALMONEE	If that is so important.
GYUNG-JUNE	Make me look like Patty.
HALMONEE	What does Patty look like?
GYUNG-JUNE	My hair—
EDWARD	Yeah.
GYUNG-JUNE	Take the colour out. Make it pale.
EDWARD	Cool.
GYUNG-JUNE	Push my face out. It's so flat. My nose.
EDWARD	It's puffy and flat.

GYUNG-JUNE	Make it look like a button. A button to kiss every night before bed. This wide face.
HALMONEE	As round as the moon.
EDWARD	Big with everything spaced out.
GYUNG-JUNE	Condense it. Bleach it. Lighten it so my hair will match my face. I want bigger eyes. Wide beautiful blue eyes like the lapis.
HALMONEE	You are colder. Your hair is ice, your eyes stone. Your face a block of marble.
EDWARD	Tough.
HALMONEE	Less penetrable.
GYUNG-JUNE	Beautiful.
HALMONEE	A matter of perspective.

Scene 17

The phone rings. MEE-GYUNG answers it and mocks the person on the other end with nonsense words.

MEE-GYUNG   Chi-chi-nee-whoa-fong-nee-too. Me no speakie no dirty Chinese. You have the wrong number.

MEE-GYUNG hangs up. The phone rings again, and she answers it in the same way.

You Chinese people are smelly. Tee-tee-now-sing-fong-fong-tee too. You Chinese people leave me alone!

> *She hangs up, and when the phone rings
> again she just looks at it.* UMMA
> *rushes into the room to answer it.*

UMMA   Yuh-bo-sae-yo? [Hello?]
Uhn-nee! [Sister!]
Ahn-yung-ha-sae-yo. [Hello.]

> *Pause.*

Woos-gee-ji-ma-sae-yo?
[Are you kidding me?]

> *She looks at* MEE-GYUNG.

Muh-yo? [Pardon?]

> *Pause.*

Ah-nee. [No.]

> *She gives* MEE-GYUNG *a look of
> displeasure, then scares her away.*

Ah-yoo! Na-bbeun-sae-gi! [Bad child!]

> *She then speaks into the phone:*

Dear sister... I've been thinking... what if—

> APBA *enters, and* UMMA *stops what
> she was saying.*

—yes, yes, everything is fine. I should go. I
have to go and make dinner. Maybe you can call
me tomorrow? Good bye, Uhn-nee. I miss you.

APBA   Your sister?

UMMA   She called me.

APBA   Did you have a good talk with her?

UMMA	She cares about me. Dinner will be ready soon.
APBA	How was your day?
UMMA	Fine. Someone at work left her husband. He came looking for her. But she wasn't there. The rest of the cleaning ladies and I think she went back to her country. She was never happy in Canada.
APBA	Sounds like a coward to me.
UMMA	I think she's pretty courageous.
APBA	Courageous? No, a selfish coward—otherwise, why would she abandon her husband and cause him such disgrace?
UMMA	She did what's best for herself. Always do what's best for you.

UMMA exits.

Scene 18

Flashback to Korea: HALMONEE *is waiting.* UMMA *enters, harried. Slides of protest scenes are projected onto the stage.*

HALMONEE	Kyung-Ma, I'm glad you didn't forget about your children.
UMMA	I'm sorry I'm late. Are the kids okay?
HALMONEE	Everyone will be fine once you stop your involvement with the Student Committee. How dare you put your whole family in danger!
UMMA	What are you talking about?

HALMONEE	Where were you tonight?
UMMA	I told you, I had a meeting at the university.
HALMONEE	You were at the demonstration.
UMMA	There were only speeches.
HALMONEE	How long have you been a member of the Student Committee?
UMMA	I'm not a member. I support what they're doing.
HALMONEE	Do you know what happens if the government sees you at these demonstrations? They arrest you and put you in jail, where you will be tortured—
UMMA	I was only listening.
HALMONEE	Think of your family.
UMMA	I am.
HALMONEE	You don't understand, do you?
UMMA	Umma, you know what the military did to our family. It's going to happen all over again. Can't you see Park Chung Hee is running a dictatorship? And he's using the threat of communism to instill fear, so Koreans will do nothing.
HALMONEE	Kyung-Ma, as long as you continue your involvement with the Student Committee, I can't call you my daughter.
UMMA	Where are the children?
HALMONEE	Sleeping in your old room.
UMMA	Fine!

Scene 19

UMMA *is cleaning up the house.*
GYUNG-JUNE *is sitting, reading* Anne
Of Green Gables.

UMMA

Messmessmessmessmess! Yes, I went through
years and years of education. I aspired to do
something with my life, to gain respect from my
family, from my co-workers, from the Canadian
people, so I can be nothing but a maidmaidmaid-
maidmaid!

> *She finds a lunch bag hidden behind a
> cabinet.*

What...? *(finds several more)* Gyung-June, what
is this?

> *She walks up to* GYUNG-JUNE *and
> shoves the bag in her face.*

What are these? Is this what you do to your
lunches?

> GYUNG-JUNE *just stares at* UMMA.

Kee-gee-bae! [Tramp!] Do I have to watch you
eat your lunches? What is wrong with you? Why
are you always hurting me?

GYUNG-JUNE

The food embarrasses me.

UMMA

Embarrasses you?

GYUNG-JUNE

It smells. It isn't normal.

UMMA

Normal? What is normal?

GYUNG-JUNE

Tuna fish.

UMMA

Tuna fish?

GYUNG-JUNE   It's what the Canadian kids eat.

UMMA   Tuna fish.

GYUNG-JUNE   Whenever I bring my lunch to school, I have to eat alone. I don't like being different. I don't like always having to tell people where I'm from. Correcting the pronunciation of my name. Getting confused with English and Korean. Being made fun of all the time. Why are we here? Do you hate me so much to take me away from the only place I know as home? Away from Halmonee?

UMMA   Gyung-June-na, let me tell you a story.

GYUNG-JUNE   About Halmonee?

UMMA   No.

GYUNG-JUNE   Umma, I don't want to hear any of your stories.

GYUNG-JUNE *walks away.* UMMA *continues to clean.*

Scene 20

Flashback to Korea: HALMONEE *is outside her home.* GYUNG-JUNE *is nine years old, and runs towards her.*

GYUNG-JUNE   Halmonee! Halmonee!

HALMONEE   Ah-suh-oh-no-rah [come here], Gyung-June-na.

GYUNG-JUNE *bows.*

GYUNG-JUNE   Ahn-yung-ha-sae-yo [hello], Halmonee.

HALMONEE   What is wrong with my Gyung-June?

GYUNG-JUNE	Your only Gyung-June!
HALMONEE	And still my favourite.
GYUNG-JUNE	Halmonee, how come you haven't visited?
HALMONEE	It is a long story. I'm glad you've come. I've missed you.
GYUNG-JUNE	I've missed you too.
HALMONEE	How is your Umma?
GYUNG-JUNE	Okay. Halmonee, what's Canada?
HALMONEE	It is a country far from here.
GYUNG-JUNE	It really is a place. What's in Canada?
HALMONEE	People. Trees. Cars. Your father's brother lives in Toronto. It is a city in Canada.
GYUNG-JUNE	Is that why we're going there?
HALMONEE	Who is going to Canada?
GYUNG-JUNE	Umma, Apba, Mee-Gyung, and... you?
HALMONEE	No.
GYUNG-JUNE	How come you're not coming with us?
HALMONEE	I don't know.
GYUNG-JUNE	Is it really far from here?
HALMONEE	Too far to walk to.
GYUNG-JUNE	They whispered something about an airplane.
HALMONEE	Yes, the best way to travel to Canada is by plane.

GYUNG-JUNE	We're not going for long, are we?
HALMONEE	I don't know, Gyung-June-na.
GYUNG-JUNE	I don't want to go!
HALMONEE	Canada is a beautiful place.
GYUNG-JUNE	Halmonee, let me stay with you. They have Mee-Gyung.
HALMONEE	They need you for Mee-Gyung. To look out for her, as the oldest should. When are you leaving?
GYUNG-JUNE	Soon, I think. It's supposed to be a secret. You won't tell anyone, will you?
HALMONEE	Who would I tell? All of you are so important to me. That will never change. Remember Gyung-June-na, I will always be with you. Distance means nothing to the heart. You are my only Gyung-June.
GYUNG-JUNE	You are my only Halmonee.
HALMONEE	Umma and Apba love you. Try not to blame them for too much.
GYUNG-JUNE	Halmonee, tell me stories. About your life. So you will never leave me and you'll continue to breathe in front of me as you are now.
HALMONEE	Gyung-June-na, you are such an interesting child. There is no time. I can teach you a song in the meantime, so you will always remember me. When you sing these words, remember the times we've shared in Korea. Don't forget where you're from. Don't forget me, Gyung-June-na.

HALMONEE *sings "Ah-Ree-Rang."*

Scene 21

UMMA *has a dream:*

UMMA	Kyung-Mei!
HALMONEE	This is where it happened.
UMMA	You never let me go to his funeral.
HALMONEE	There was nothing to see. He was blown away.

HALMONEE *starts to exit.* GYUNG-JUNE *runs up to her.*

GYUNG-JUNE	Halmonee, please tell me stories. So I can understand what it's like to be Korean.

HALMONEE *drops a white rose and exits. "Ah-Ree-Rang" is heard in the background.*

UMMA	There were six children in my family. All but two are in Korea—the two youngest. Me and a brother. *(points to* MEE-GYUNG, *who is playing* KYUNG-MEI*)* His name is Kyung-Mei. *(points to* GYUNG-JUNE, *who is playing* KYUNG-MA, *reading a book)* My name is Kyung-Ma. Every summer, the family would have vacations on a beautiful island.
KYUNG-MEI	Kyung-Ma, look at what I found. Are they not beau-ti-ful? Look how they catch the light. Spark! Now it's gone.
KYUNG-MA	Those are bullet shells. Don't touch them, Kyung-Mei.

KYUNG-MA *goes back to reading her book.*

KYUNG-MEI	There are so many different kinds. From different countries. Here's one from—please read it to me.

KYUNG-MA	They all say the same thing, only in different languages. They don't say, "Made in blank blank country."
KYUNG-MEI	How do you know?
KYUNG-MA	Okay. Fine. Have it your way. *(pretends to read the bullet shells)* Let's see... this one is from France.
KYUNG-MEI	And this one's from Ca-na-da, and here's one from U.S.S.R. Kyung-Ma, what's it like to be a soldier?
KYUNG-MA	I don't know.
KYUNG-MEI	I'm going to find one.

> KYUNG-MEI *runs off stage.* UMMA
> *walks across the stage, picks up the*
> *bullet shells, kisses then, then puts*
> *them in her pocket.* KYUNG-MEI
> *returns with a stick, pretending it is a*
> *gun. He practices holding the stick in a*
> *gun position. A young* WHITE DOG
> *looks on, then runs across the stage.*

WHITE DOG	*(pretending)* Oww! You shot me! Pain. Pain. *(KYUNG-MEI starts laughing)* Everywhere. Terrible pain—hey, why are you laughing?
KYUNG-MEI	You're pretending.
WHITE DOG	Play with me, kid. *(pretending)* Ohhh! Owww! My heart! My heart!
KYUNG-MEI	Fine, I'll take you to the butcher.

> WHITE DOG *jumps up.*

WHITE DOG	What!
KYUNG-MEI	Faker.

WHITE DOG	*(offers his paw)* White Dog. Please to meet you.
KYUNG-MEI	Kyung-Mei. White Dog, do you know any soldiers?
WHITE DOG	I'm a soldier. I'm anything you want to be, so long as you take me home.
KYUNG-MEI	First, show me a real soldier.

> KYUNG-MEI *and* WHITE DOG *search all over for a soldier.*
>
> *A* NORTH KOREAN SOLDIER *enters, tattered and dirty. He dances a short, rural peasant dance to show poverty and despair. By the time* KYUNG-MEI *and* WHITE DOG *approach the* SOLDIER, *the dance should be more like stylistic, ritual exercises.*

KYUNG-MEI	Are you a soldier?
SOLDIER	*(to* KYUNG-MEI*)* The best.
KYUNG-MEI	How do I know you're a real soldier?
SOLDIER	I can teach you to be a soldier. In my secret place. Only for today.
KYUNG-MEI	*(running to* KYUNG-MA*)* Kyung-Ma, I found a real soldier! And he said he'll show me his secret place. Can I go? Please?

> KYUNG-MA *is preoccupied with her book and doesn't even look up.*

KYUNG-MA	Just don't go too far.
WHITE DOG	Hey, tell her about me!
KYUNG-MEI	And I got a pet. For all of us. Isn't he cute?

KYUNG-MA	*(head down)* Have fun.
KYUNG-MEI	*(throwing down his stick)* Hold my stick. I'm going to be using a real gun!

> KYUNG-MEI *and* WHITE DOG *run to the* SOLDIER. UMMA *walks across the stage and picks up the stick.*

SOLDIER	Some people live in ignorance. They choose to maintain systems and values of dated tradition and fight against natural progression. That's why we have bullet shells littering our beaches.
WHITE DOG	*(to* KYUNG-MEI*)* Do you understand him?
KYUNG-MEI	No, but he let me touch his gun.
SOLDIER	War is good. It reminds us humans what our natural instincts are. Simply drawing a line to separate north *(indicates himself)* from south *(indicates* KYUNG-MEI*)* won't separate us emotionally. *(points to* KYUNG-MEI*)* You. Draw a line down your centre. Right down. Now!

> *The* SOLDIER *caresses* KYUNG-MEI *with his gun.* WHITE DOG *starts to bark, and the* SOLDIER *hits him.* WHITE DOG *becomes silent.*

What happens if half the body is gone? You die. What sort of reality is half a body? Half a country? *(pause)* You draw a pretty good line.

> *No line has been drawn.* WHITE DOG *tries to bite the* SOLDIER, *who fights back and almost shoots* WHITE DOG *before* WHITE DOG *escapes.* KYUNG-MEI *is frozen.*

You stay here. I have a surprise for you.

> *The* SOLDIER *exits. An explosion is heard, and the lighting imitates a bomb exploding.* KYUNG-MEI *is blown-up stylistically, while* UMMA *and* KYUNG-MA *watch. The lighting effect continues until the end of the scene.*

UMMA Firecrackers.

KYUNG-MA Firecrackers.

UMMA
KYUNG-MA *(together)* What beautiful firecrackers.

KYUNG-MA Kyung-Mei, come and look at the sky.

UMMA Kyung-Mei.

KYUNG-MA Stop hiding.

UMMA Kyung-Mei.

KYUNG-MA Kyung-Mei!

UMMA
KYUNG-MA *(together)* Kyung-Mei!

> *The dream moves forward in time.* HALMONEE *enters.*

HALMONEE It's time to leave, everyone.

UMMA I'm ready.

HALMONEE Kyung-Ma, you can't come to the funeral. You're too young.

UMMA Umma, he's still inside the cave.

HALMONEE Don't upset me. Stay here with your mother. Now we must go.

UMMA   Umma. Umma!
                       Nah-do chuck-ko-ship-uh-yo.
                       Nah-do chuck-ko-ship-uh-yo.
                       [I want to die. I want to die.]

HALMONEE   I want to die too.

                                     HALMONEE *exits, then* KYUNG-MA.
                                     UMMA *takes the bullet shells from her
                                     pocket.*

UMMA   Let's see. This one's from France. Are they not
                       beau-ti-ful? Spark. Look how they catch the
                       light.

                                     Crying, UMMA *slowly begins to pack
                                     her suitcase. The lighting effect is
                                     transformed into a sunrise.*

Scene 22

                                     Sunrise. APBA *is just about to leave
                                     for work.* UMMA *is sitting in the
                                     kitchen, waiting for him. She has one
                                     suitcase with her.*

APBA   Why are you up? (UMMA *doesn't respond*) Yo
                       bau? Anything wrong? You have to get over this
                       sadness.

UMMA   I'm going on a trip.

APBA   Tell me this tomorrow. I've got to go to work.

UMMA   I'm leaving. I'm going back to Korea. Do you
                       care?

APBA   I'll start caring when you stop acting crazy.

UMMA	There are frozen dinners in the freezer for the children and you. The fridge is stocked with all the Canadian food everyone loves. No more Korean crap for the family.
APBA	What is happening?
UMMA	I'm doing what I have to do.
APBA	Yo bau.
UMMA	I have died too.

Pause.

APBA	When are you coming back?
UMMA	I don't know.

Scene 23

UMMA *is in the children's bedroom to say goodbye.* GYUNG-JUNE *wakes up.*

GYUNG-JUNE	Umma, I had a dream that we were back in Korea. And everyone was waiting for us at the airport—Hyuck-Dong, White Dog, and even Halmonee. They were so happy to see us again.
UMMA	Shhh. Gyung-June, go back to sleep. It was just a dream.
GYUNG-JUNE	Umma, how come you're crying?
UMMA	I love you. That's why. Go to sleep, Gyung-June-na. I'm sorry I woke you up. Be a good girl and take care of Apba and Mee-Gyung. Go to sleep, Gyung-June-na. Go to sleep.
GYUNG-JUNE	Umma, where are you going?

UMMA	To Korea.
GYUNG-JUNE	Umma?
UMMA	I'm sorry.
GYUNG-JUNE	Can I go with you?
UMMA	You want to come with me? Gyung-June... I can't. I can't take you with me. I don't have enough money. I don't. I'm sorry. I'm sorry. Gyung-June-na, you belong here.
GYUNG-JUNE	I don't belong anywhere.

Scene 24

APBA *enters the children's bedroom.*

APBA	Gyung-June-na, you're up. Wake Mee-Gyung up, wake her up and we'll all go to McDonald's.
GYUNG-JUNE	I'm not going to McDonald's. I'm not going to Korea. All I'm going to do is stay here. I hate you!

GYUNG-JUNE *starts to exit, but* APBA *stops her.*

APBA	No! I'm not going to lose you too.

Pause.

GYUNG-JUNE	Wake up, Mee-Gyung.
APBA	Mee-Gyung-a, I want to take you somewhere.

MEE-GYUNG *wakes up.*

MEE-GYUNG	Apba?

APBA	Do you like McDonald's? Let's go to McDonald's. We can go to all the McDonald's in the city.
MEE-GYUNG	What's the catch?
APBA	Come on, hurry up. Get dressed.
MEE-GYUNG	Apba, how come you're crying?
APBA	Because I have two beautiful daughters. I am so lucky.
MEE-GYUNG	Apba, where's Umma?
	She looks at GYUNG-JUNE. APBA *and* GYUNG-JUNE *do not respond.*

Scene 25

	APBA, MEE-GYUNG, *and* GYUNG-JUNE *at McDonald's.*
MEE-GYUNG	Apba, I can't eat anymore. I should be at school.
APBA	Just finish your hamburger, Mee-Gyung-a. Please.
	WHITE DOG *enters, carrying a gun. Only* MEE-GYUNG *can see him.*
WHITE DOG	*(to* MEE-GYUNG*)* Hey! I want to greet your father.
MEE-GYUNG	I'm warning you—my father's weird. He's weirder today than he normally is.
WHITE DOG	I get along with all sorts.
MEE-GYUNG	We'll see. Apba, White Dog wants to say hi.

WHITE DOG *bows to* APBA.

WHITE DOG	Ahn-yung-ha-sae-yo. [Hello.]
APBA	Mee-Gyung, stop playing games. Eat your hamburger.
WHITE DOG	What's his problem?
MEE-GYUNG	Umma left today.
WHITE DOG	That's too bad.
MEE-GYUNG	I don't care. *(takes the gun from* WHITE DOG*)* He doesn't need her with me around.
WHITE DOG	Walk low so they can't see you. Hold your gun hard.
MEE-GYUNG	I'll kill anyone who hurts my father. Pow!
WHITE DOG	Why did she leave?
MEE-GYUNG	She's a weakling!
WHITE DOG	How come she didn't take you?
MEE-GYUNG	Stop asking stupid questions!
WHITE DOG	You're angry because she didn't take you with her.
MEE-GYUNG	I'm not angry! I hate her.
WHITE DOG	Don't say that.
MEE-GYUNG	It's true.
WHITE DOG	Hate makes people crazy.
MEE-GYUNG	Apba, you won't leave me, will you?

APBA   No, Mee-Gyung-a. You are my youngest daughter.

MEE-GYUNG   Good. We'll do fine then.

> MEE-GYUNG *salutes* WHITE DOG.
> WHITE DOG *salutes* MEE-GYUNG.

Scene 26

> GYUNG-JUNE's *dream. She runs towards* HALMONEE's *house.*

GYUNG-JUNE   Halmonee! Halmonee!

HALMONEE   Gyung-June-na, come inside and stop yelling.

GYUNG-JUNE   Halmonee, I've missed you.

HALMONEE   Ah, my Gyung-June.

GYUNG-JUNE   Your only Gyung-June.

HALMONEE   Yes, yes, yes. My only Gyung-June. *(she gives her a red rose)* Here is a flower for my only Gyung-June. Now tell me—how are Umma, Apba, and Mee-Gyung?

GYUNG-JUNE   Halmonee, Umma left us.

HALMONEE   Your mother always does what she wants to do.

GYUNG-JUNE   Why didn't she take me? I belong in Korea with you.

HALMONEE   But I do not belong to your world. *(she gives her a white rose)* Love the country you are destined to live in.

GYUNG-JUNE   My destiny is in Korea. Isn't it?

HALMONEE	I have to go back to my home.

> HALMONEE *walks along a line, then is sprayed with bullets and falls.*

GYUNG-JUNE	Halmonee!
HALMONEE	Go be with Apba and Mee-Gyung.
GYUNG-JUNE	I belong with you.
HALMONEE	You know in your heart where you belong.

> *Pause.*

GYUNG-JUNE	Halmonee, jung-mal-sah-rang-hae-yo. [I really love you.]
HALMONEE	Gyung-June-na, I love you too.

Scene 27

> MEE-GYUNG *and* GYUNG-JUNE *in their bedroom.*

MEE-GYUNG	Cah, can I talk with you?
GYUNG-JUNE	Sure.
MEE-GYUNG	Do you think Umma is coming back?
GYUNG-JUNE	I don't know.
MEE-GYUNG	I don't want her to come back.
GYUNG-JUNE	If she does, she's still our mother.

> *Pause.*

MEE-GYUNG	Cah, I'm scared.

GYUNG-JUNE   Me too. *(pause)* Mee-Gyung, can I tell you a story?

MEE-GYUNG   About White Dog?

GYUNG-JUNE   No.

MEE-GYUNG   About Umma?

GYUNG-JUNE   Yes. About Umma.

The lights begin to fade.

Once upon a time, there was an older sister, Kyung-Ma. And she had a younger brother, Kyung-Mei. This was Kyung-Ma's favourite story....

Lights down.

The End.